Found & Lost

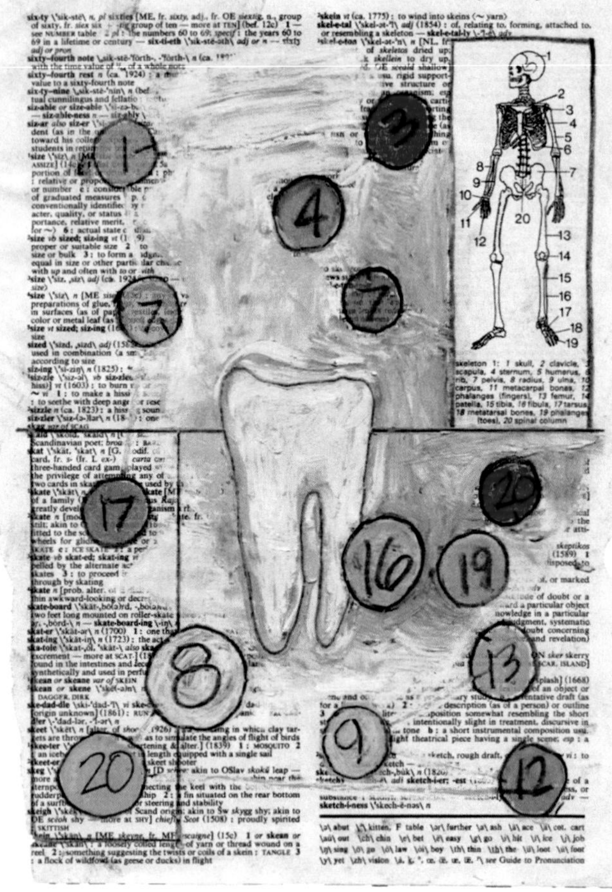

sixty • sketchy 1103
²skein vt (ca. 1775) : to wind into skeins (~ yarn)
skel·e·tal \'skel-ə-tᵊl\ adj (1854) : of, relating to, forming, attached to, or resembling a skeleton — skel·e·tal·ly
sketch·i·ness \'skech-ē-nəs\ n

FOUND
&
LOST

POEMS & ART

George McKim

SILVER BIRCH PRESS
LOS ANGELES, CALIFORNIA

Published by Silver Birch Press

ISBN-13: 978-0692399156

ISBN-10: 0692399151

First Edition: August 2015

Email: silver@silverbirchpress.com

Web: silverbirchpress.com

Blog: silverbirchpress.wordpress.com

Mailing Address:
Silver Birch Press
P.O. Box 29458
Los Angeles, CA 90029

Cover: donkey by George McKim

Frontispiece: skeleton by George McKim

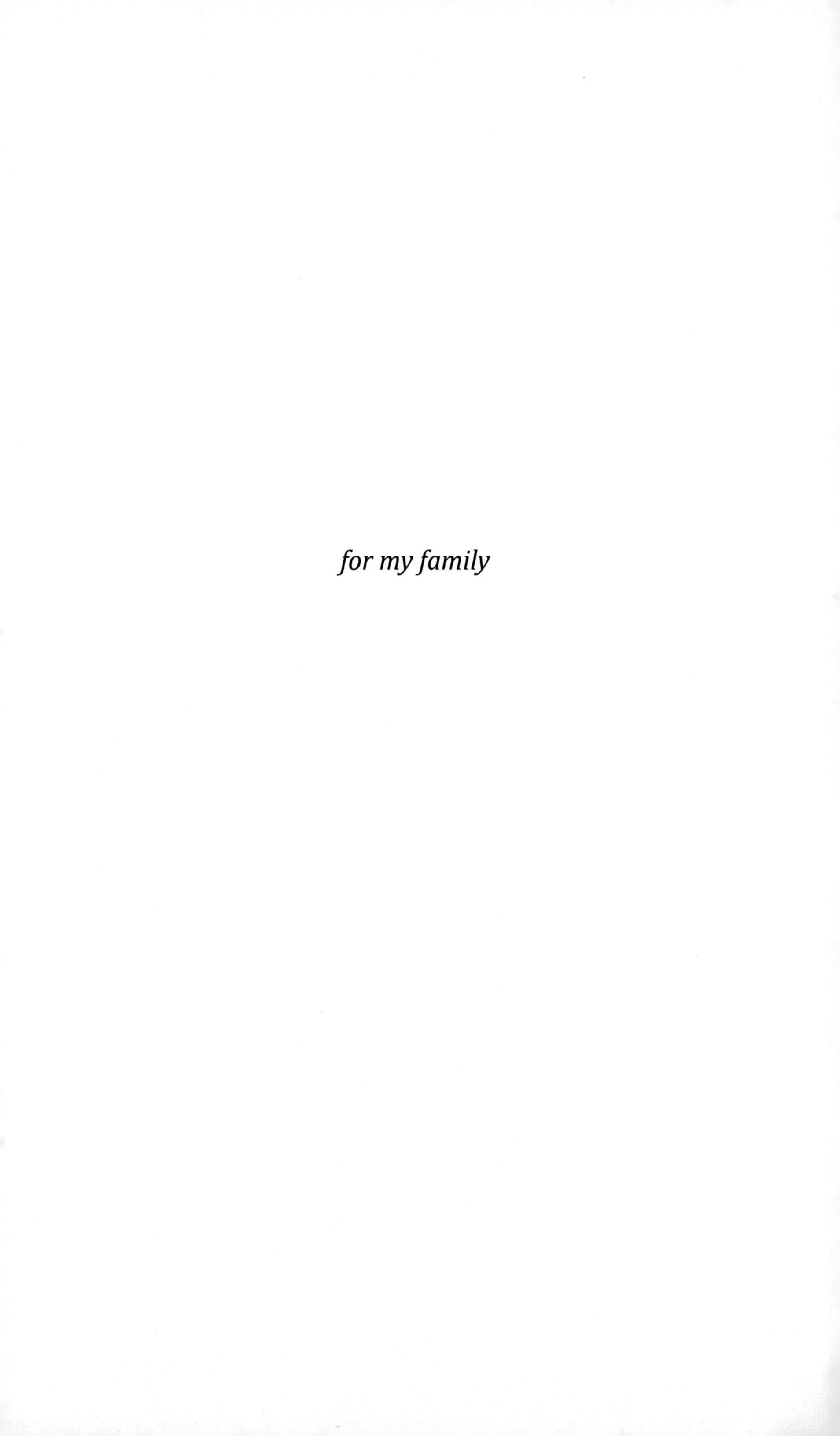

for my family

Introduction

George McKim

"Poetry can communicate before it is understood." *T.S Eliot*

"Poetry's purpose is to use language itself as music." *Anonymous*

"Poetry is not the record of an event, it is an event." *Robert Lowell*

When I was a graduate student in art school in 1984, Tom Phillips was a visiting artist. His book *A Humament* was my first exposure to Found Poetry. Twenty-three years later, at the age of fifty-six, I began writing poetry.

In April 2013, I was one of eighty-five poets selected to create Found Poetry from one of eighty-five Pulitzer-Prize-winning novels in the *Found Poetry Review's* project—"Pulitzer Remix." That project was the inspiration for the poems in this chapbook. It was through that project, and the interaction with other participating poets, that I learned what Found Poetry is all about.

After Pulitzer Remix, I spent several months writing Found Poems repurposed from the poetry of other contemporary poets and remixed into these Found Poems. The writing process for me was to read each poem and select as many interesting words as possible, and it was the chance relationships among these randomly selected words that sparked ideas for these poems. Rather than bringing an agenda to the creative process, I let the poems tell me what they wanted to be. These poems are collages.

The artwork in this book is not an illustration of the poetry—it's a parallel universe, and there to cleanse the palate between poems.

The "remix," for instance, appears as a meta-modern form because it allows a single author to interact honestly and responsibly with the language of another with the aim of creating a new, unique, cohesive, coherent, and entirely "whole" self-expression. A poststructuralist would never remix a pop song into this sort of arrangement of language (that is, "a new, unique, cohesive, coherent, and entirely whole self-expression") because to do so would suggest that once language has been taken apart beyond all recognition it can be put back together again in a way that is meaningful and even aesthetically pleasing for us and large numbers of others. Moreover, the metamodern remix suggests that reconstituting broken language—even language the author broke herself—is a fundamentally optimistic and even moral act, as it models for us (and perhaps others) that we can, indeed, live "as if things that are broken are capable of being mended . . ." (Seth Abramson, *Metamodernism: the Basics III)*

Table of Contents

AUTHOR'S NOTE

The poems and artwork in this book are in the forms of Found Poetry and Visual Poetry.

Found Poetry is a poetic form comprised of words and lines taken from other sources. In this book, the text in the Found Poems is taken from poems by other poets. Though poets often borrow lines from other poets and mix them in with their own, a true Found Poem is composed entirely of text from other sources. The Found Poems in this book are similar to Cento Poems, except Cento Poems use entire lines from other poems, not words and parts of lines.

Visual Poetry, or Vispo, is poetry or visual art in which the visual arrangement of text, images, and symbols is important in conveying the intended effect of the work. It is sometimes referred to as concrete poetry, a term that predates visual poetry and was once synonymous with it. Visual poetry work tends to blur the distinctions between different media, and blurs the distinction between art and text. Whereas concrete poetry is still recognizable as poetry, since it is composed of purely typographic elements, visual poetry is generally much less text-dependent. Visual poems incorporate text, but the text may have primarily a visual function. Visual poems often incorporate significant amounts of non-text imagery in addition to text.

Found & Lost

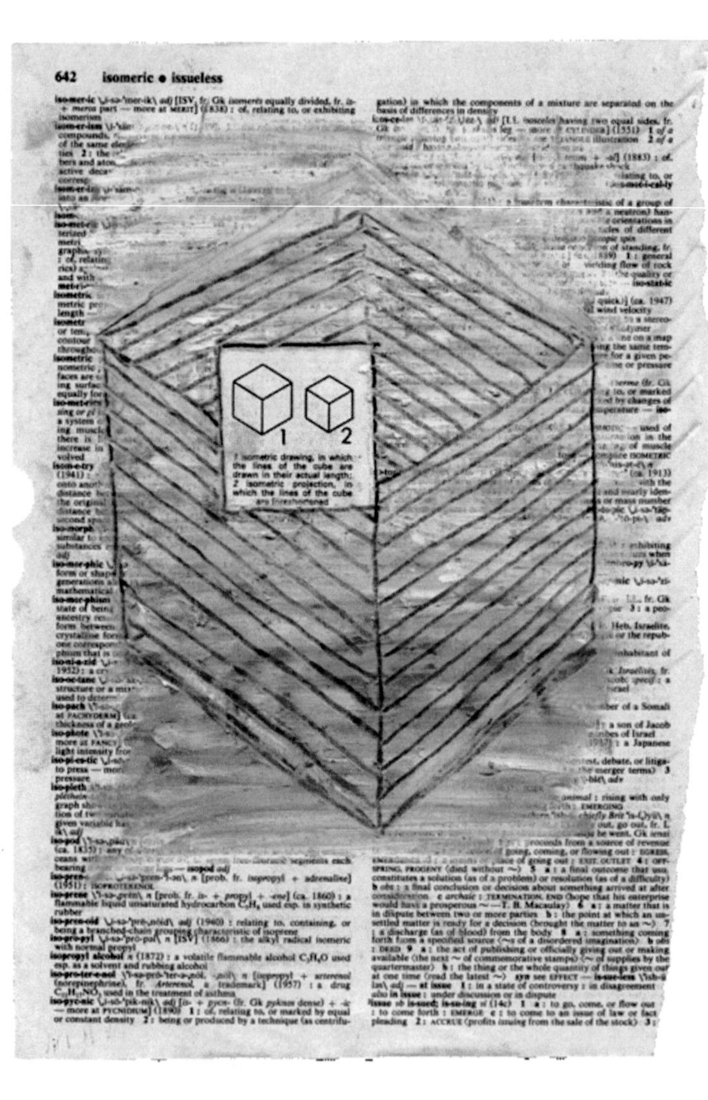
642 isomeric • issueless
1
2
1 isometric drawing, in which the lines of the cube are drawn in their actual length; 2 isometric projection, in which the lines of the cube are foreshortened

that thing which is singing
(for jackson maclow)

a city a land. land.
it is that
curious empty length.

that thing which everything trembling
is even temporarily sudden and standing.

a sullenness
a nervous light

just summer,
that thing which is singing and
showing its hair

a city a thick. speech.
a shining. monstrous. reckless music

that thing which is winter. circular. aching.
neglected. repeated.

a city a narrow, grainy light
makes morning darker, cracked
inside that curious
empty length.

SOURCE TEXT BY JACKSON MACLOW
call me ishmael
stein 100: a feather likeness of the justice chair

white if white
(for gertrude stein)

either six nine or
fourteen daisies a hat

or a hat or a day
i add added it to it.

trembling and
not even trembling,

is kind of a song a green kind of
green a green and nothing and
nothing and nothing round, nothing

strangely cut. cut in white,
cut in white is a beginning and an end
to beginning. is not only white but

white if white is a single color
and not that that is red that
is the glittering disease and a red

thing not a round thing but a white thing,
a red thing and a white thing. a white way
of being round is something

white lilies are lily white
there is a sweetness in the lamp
and the cake and the white noise

SOURCE TEXT BY GERTRUDE STEIN
stanzas in meditation
tender buttons [a plate]
tender buttons [objects]

in the yawn light
(for bob hicok)

a horse eating
the yawn light

the baby sleeps
swallowed by the meter of the sea.

we were. a woman
in the yawn light

not a woman
but the anguish of the house
keeping secrets
in the marriage of light

fire is the basis for all forms of the mouth.
the river reads its poem

because I suddenly dream of horses
a sky of starlings flow like cursive

it's not fire but my eyes as shadows
pushed to the window anyway

our hands, that hold us in their windows
nostalgic for the touch of

a horse eating
the yawn light

SOURCE TEXT BY BOB HICOK
epithalamium
in michael robin's class minus one
go greyhound

a blackish field
(for paul celan)

steps out of the stars
dig a grave for the dance

black milk when
your golden hair your ashen hair

a grave in the breezes
sing your black milk eyes

a grave in the air
death is your golden hair
your ashen hair

the stone in the air
your eye adds petals to it

and hammers
a blackish field, the
stars ask after you

you are ash
ash, ash.

night.
a green silence

petrified
psalms,
the conversations
of the unmistakable grass

SOURCE TEXT BY PAUL CELAN
death fugue
flower the straitening

dole 239 doom
dole (dōl), 1. a portion of
summer
don key
Donkey (3 ft. high at the shoulder)
hat, āge, cãre, fär; let, bē, tėrm; it, ice; hot, ōpen, ôrder; oil, out; cup, put, rüle, ūse; takən

a damp, orange
(for zachary hamilton)

at ten o'clock
a window
growing a pathway
in empty fur

drifting in
these shadows
reach for the wooden ladder
of morning

hands
leaking from a house

are the only serpents
in the county-fair

sun
overflowed from the sunlight alleyway
through the fiber-optic birds

the edge blur distance
a damp, orange

satellite

SOURCE TEXT BY ZACHARY HAMILTON
share your satellite with me

like a heart run down
(for michael ryan)

one hundred thousand mornings
their odd music
slumped like light,

from what throat,
the song in it?

the body
ends in rain
in a dim room

in a planetarium.
fake stars
their muscles slack
like a heart run down,

after there's nothing,
like a beautiful song
from the skin

SOURCE TEXT BY MICHAEL RYAN
poem at thirty
my bright aluminum tumblers
the past
sex

i did not invent america
(for lawrence ferlinghetti)

in the sad plethora of afternoon

in stationwagons
in drunken doorways
too narrow

i may be moving to detroit
with the garbagemen in the rain
that sound like every day

ben shahn painted them
when it was snowing

i am leading a quiet life

i did not invent america
i did not invent the clouds
i did not invent weeping
i did not invent war
i did not invent hotdogs
i did not invent the sun
i did not invent brooklyn
i did not invent tom sawyer
i did not invent the yellow pages
i did not invent detroit
i did not invent yellow hair
i did not invent fifth avenue
i did not invent flannel trousers
i did not invent the rain
i did not invent love

in the plethora of afternoon

SOURCE TEXT BY LAWRENCE FERLINGHETTI
autobiography

immerse
342
imperative
imp
Imp

a strange song
(for ee cummings and federico garcia lorca)

spring
keeps all its blood
inside my lips

little friend of
a strange song

wind it up it
like a perhaps
moon

tic clocks toc
springs wheels
inside of
everywhere

SOURCE TEXT
spring is like a perhaps hand by ee cummings
9. by ee cummings
gacela of the dark death by federico garcia lorca

judgment 367 junk
junk
3. person chosen to settle a dispute or to decide who wins a race, etc. 4. settle (a dispute); decide on the winner in a race, a debate, etc.
mixed-up mess; state of confusion. jum bled, jum bling.
jug gler (jug′lər),
juice (jüs), 1. the liquid part of
juices of the stomach help to digest
Ju ly (jü lī′), the seventh month of
year. It has 31 days. Ju lies.
jum ble (jum′bəl), 1. mix or confuse:
She jumbled up everything in her drawer while hunting for her white gloves. 2. a muddle;
hat, āge, cãre, fär; let, bē, tėrm; it, īce; hot, ōpen, ôrder; oil, out; cup, pút, rüle, ūse; takən

under the endless blinkings of eyes
(for tristan tzara and james wright)

the light has come home
drunk from the sea

rises in your throat

a bluejay
with its tin eyes
staggers into the night

stars have galloped
from the trees

half drunk
the roof crumbles away

under the endless
blinkings of eyes

i have been dreaming

SOURCE TEXT
on the road of the stars by tristan tzara
two hangovers by james wright

a ruse
(for will alexander)

here i am
posing in a mirror of paper

drained of
fallen snow

a bloodless sun
a collision
a ruse
a conspiracy
a merciless curvature of chamber lilies
a centripetal wave of isochronous paratactic distortion

syllables scrawled in a totem of glints

SOURCE TEXT BY WILL ALEXANDER
above the human nerve domain
apprenticeship

jet
365
join

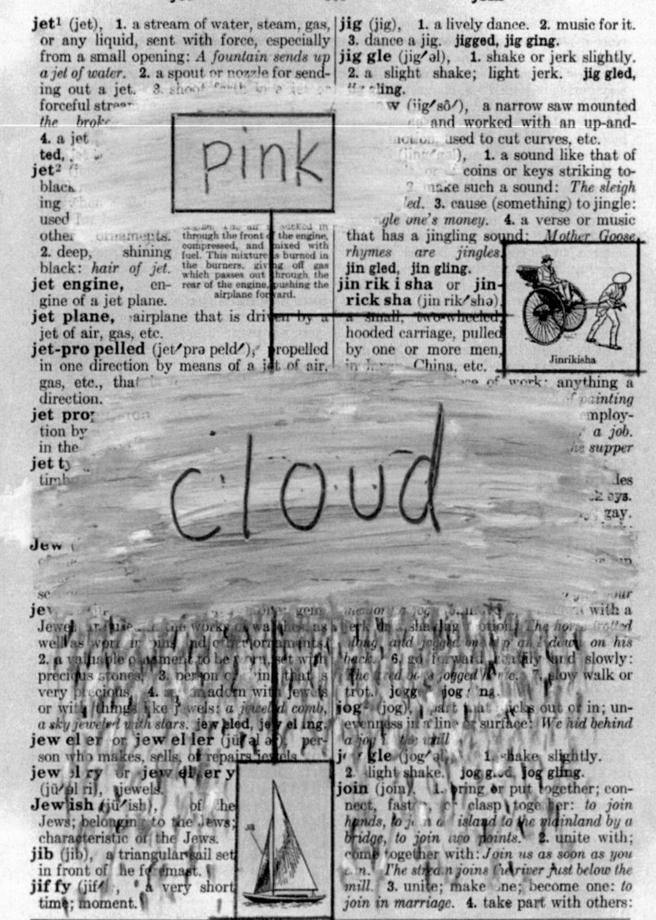
pink
cloud

i dream you an abstract field
(for ron silliman)

jet trails in cloud wisps

this untrimmed garden
shadows sit still
something bell-shaped,
nameless

dandelion
their light with
something
unnamable
inconsolable
surrounding the heart

rises from the river
among rebellion
what winnowing

from the first book to
the nest the sun
in cloud language
what music crossing into
the deaf autumn place

pink driven through the streets
one millisecond of stillness

great raft of a bed
for days the geography
in your former home

only the apocalypse
beneath the fifth bridge
the painter goes pale
smile still shines but

a new sun as vicious as
the early train,
just outlines

cut from the paper
my dreams
then, i dream you
an abstract field

it's 6:11 am
upstairs a faucet turns
briefly but not the wind, wind
up an old clock
with a different bird song
for every hour,

birds finally
begin to twitter
particular trumpet,
said to contain

the blue
unimaginable

against the water
wild but for the binding stitched
deep into the notebook's spine

SOURCE TEXT BY RON SILLIMAN
revelator

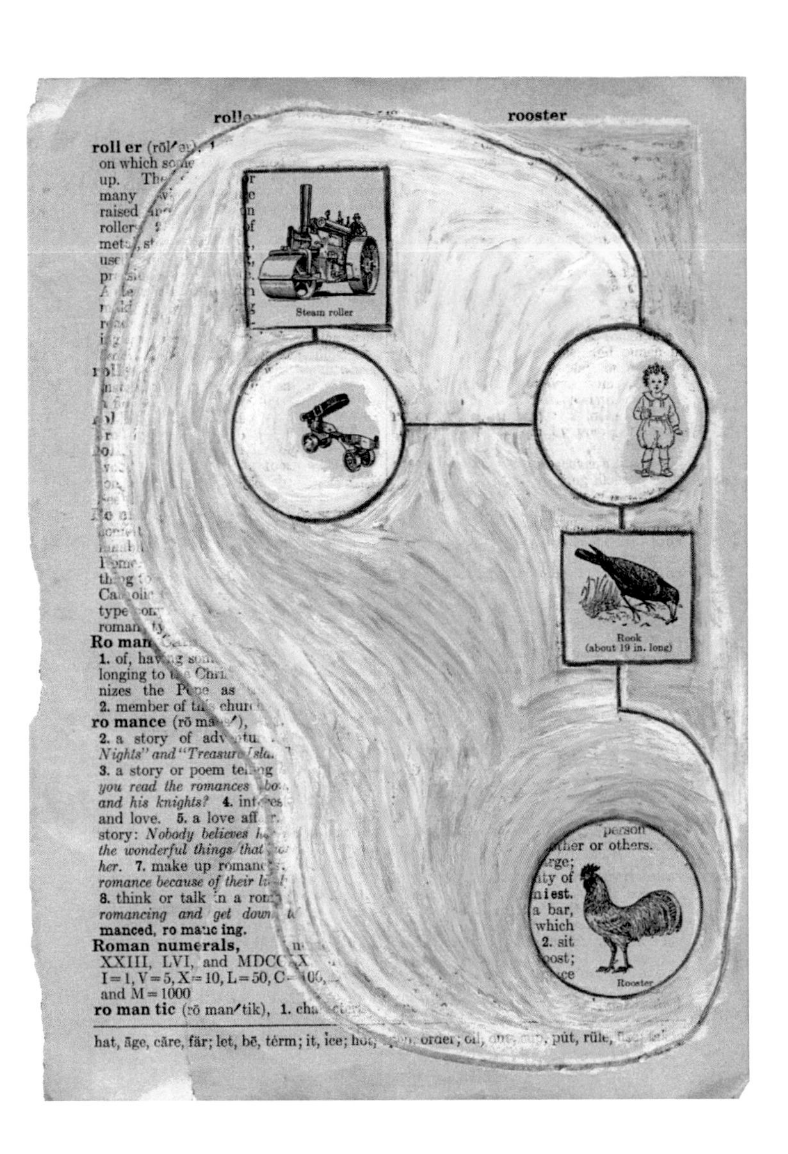
rooster
roll er (rōl′ər).
on which so
up.
many
raised
rollers
Steam roller
Ro man
1. of, ha
longing to
nizes the
as
2. member of
ro mance (rō ma
2. a story of adv
Nights" and "Treasure Isla
3. a story or poem te
you read the romances
and his knights? 4. int
and love. 5. a love af
story: Nobody believes
the wonderful things that
her. 7. make up roman
romance because of their
8. think or talk in a ro
romancing and get down
manced, ro manc ing.
Roman numerals,
XXIII, LVI, and MDCC
I = 1, V = 5, X = 10, L = 50, C = 100,
and M = 1000
ro man tic (rō man′tik), 1. cha
Rook
(about 19 in. long)
person
other or others.
Rooster
hat, āge, cãre, fär; let, bē, tėrm; it, īce; hot, order; oil, pu̇t, rüle,

slanted against morning
(for emily dickinson and yusef komunyakaa)

in the black mirror
a lane of yellow
a red bird's
wings cutting across my stare

bird the silence his eyes
look through mine
the wall

a window
inside the stone
in the black mirror

no, the sky
a plane in the sky silver
impossible bird

slanted against morning
i turn again,
depending on the light
my reflection

inside the granite night
my black face fades

i'm trying to erase
the 58,022 names in the
vietnam memorial

SOURCE TEXT
a lane of yellow led the eye by emily dickinson
a bird came down the walk by emily dickinson
facing it by yusef komunyakaa

because the sun
(for will alexander)

from flesh
the cellular dove

implanted
with a green umber sound

because the sun
sings at a certain pitch
beyond the potter's field

sings
beyond the blood

SOURCE TEXT BY WILL ALEXANDER
the improbable brush fire singer

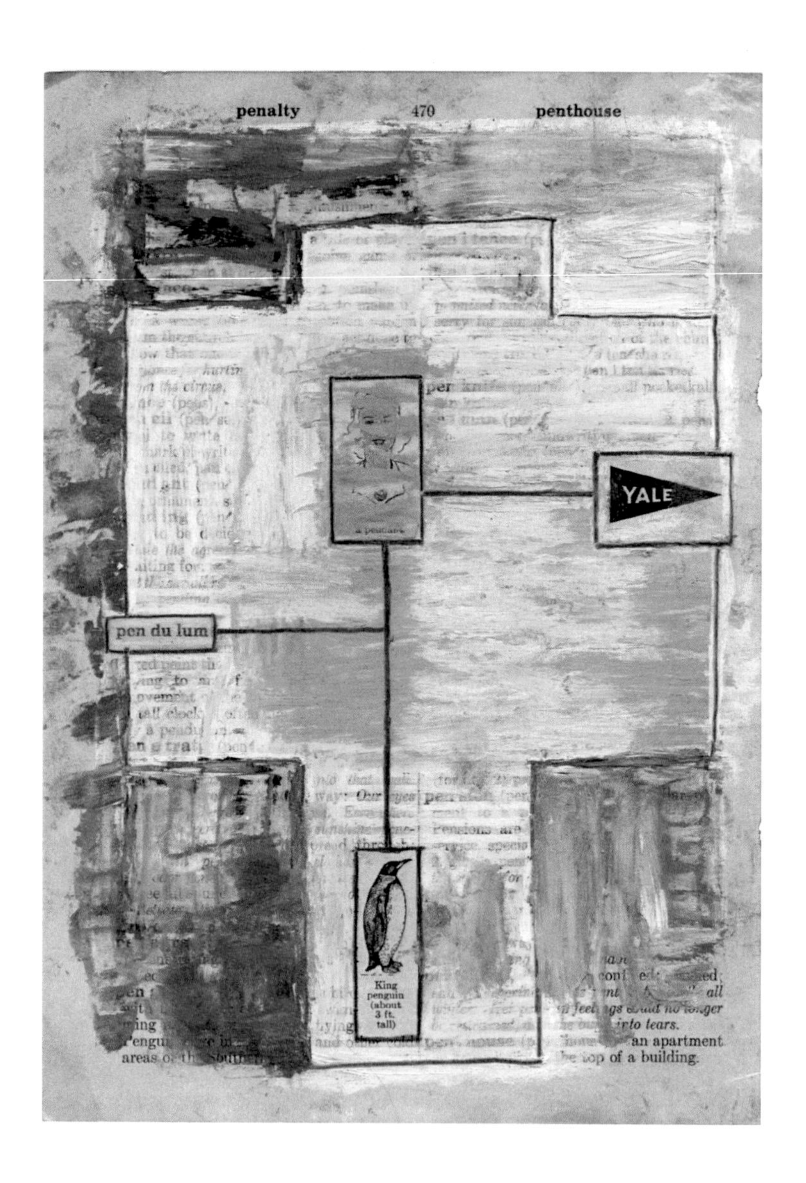
penalty
470
penthouse
pen du lum
YALE
King penguin (about 3 ft. tall)
into tears.
an apartment
top of a building.

you wait in the snow-drift electricity
(for james wright, tristan tzara and charles bukowski)

i walked about the town
i walked, like a folded bird

a tiny bird bathed in a bowl of air
at our house the clock flowers
looped in a yoke of darkened garden

weeping for loneliness
you wait in the snow-drift electricity
but then a girl appeared,
to wash her hair

you wait in the snow-drift electricity
for the slow fluting doves
and the sadness becomes so great

but then a girl appeared
lifting her arms
to loosen the soft braids

SOURCE TEXT
the angel by james wright
the great lament over my obscurity by tristan tzara
consummation of grief by charles bukowski

the machine's ambling spring
(for tristan tzara)

let us always
catch fire

where the rain falls with sharp eyes
where the machine's starry warmth enslaves you

let us always
catch fire
in the machine's ambling spring

where the distant river of the dead
have no home

SOURCE TEXT BY TRISTAN TZARA
Cinema Calendar Of The Abstract Heart—09
The Great Lament Of My Obscurity Three
Vegetable Swallow

grown dull
(for hart crane and don van vliet)

stars
crept across
this silence

wide from
the dice of
heartbeat
bones

without sound
without bells

grown dull in the
calyx of death's
fabulous shadow

SOURCE TEXT
at melville's tomb by hart crane
interior by hart crane
heartbeat missiles by don van vliet
the smith that cleans our stars by don van vliet

mother 423 mountain
moth er (muTH′ər), 1. female parent. 2. take care of: She mothers her baby sister. 3. the cause or source of anything. 4. the head of a large community of religious women.
moth er hood (muTH′ər hůd), 1. state of being a mother: The young wife was proud of her motherhood. 2. qualities of a mother.
the
and or wife. moth-
moth er ly (muTH′ər li), like a mother
mo tor car
mo tor cy cle
like a bicycle
a motor.
mo tor ist
ist), person
especially
does it
mo tor ize
iz), 1. furnish
motor. 2. supply
place of
ized,
1. man who
2. man
cloud
hat, āge, cãre, fär; let, bē, tėrm; it, īce; hot, ōpen, ôrder; oil, out; cup, pu̇t, rüle, ūse; takən

i was a saw of anything
(for lyn hejinian)

clouds
a sound

it will not sadly happily
my tiny words of no world

a surrounding who
swarming with music

in that unscrolling woods
i was a saw of anything

just a mouth
this room

birds adrift a shining
springs from its own shadow

sky which is now vacant
i know you only in laughing

SOURCE TEXT BY LYN HEJINIAN
happily [excerpt]

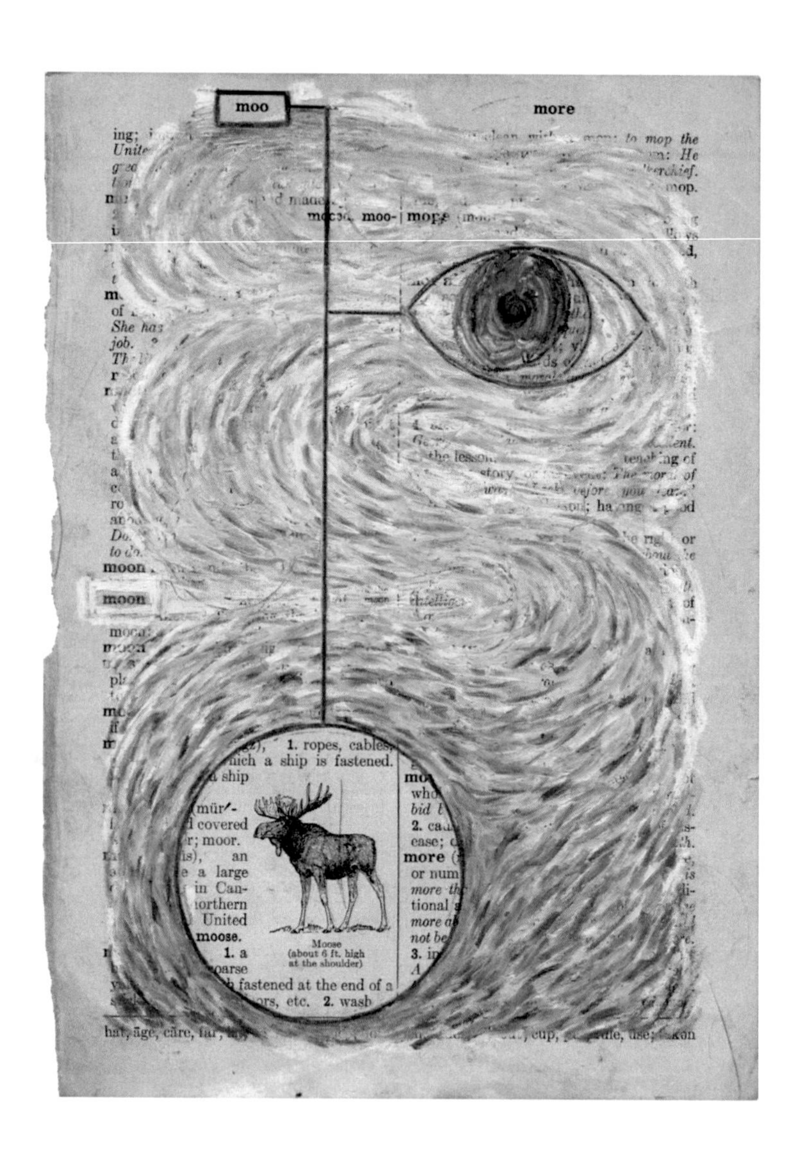
moo
more
moon
Moose
(about 6 ft. high
at the shoulder)

the dim known street
(for clark coolidge)

here the shadow has more waiting

beyond
where the sun

a stem of grey

breezy curtains of smoke

blurry shoes as I reel
in the wind of
the dim known street

the driveway is dark with
the wind of the sun

how far askance I've been

SOURCE TEXT BY CLARK COOLIDGE
album—a runthru

fever
(for danika stegeman)

artificial
music

phone ringing
like a rearview mirror

start over

patsy cline
you nod and
everything shakes and
we are trying to see into the dark

i tell you
the fever
will bleed out

we start a fire of creepy music
everything shakes

the jungle is full of knives

SOURCE TEXT BY DANIKA STEGEMAN
tabula rasa
walkabout

nervous
433
new
nerv ous (nėr′vəs), 1. of the nerves. The
brain is a part of the nervous system of th
human body. 2. easily excited or upset.
person who has been
become nervous.
timid: She is
at night. 4. strong
painted with quick
nerv ous ness (nėr
ous; being easily ups
her nervousness
nest (nest),
thing like a
(net), 1. remaining after deductions;
n deductions. A net gain or profit
tual gain after all working expenses
Nettle
Wasp's nest
Tennis net
net is used in the game of tennis.
made of very fine net. 2. a lacelike cloth.
3. a trap or snare: The guilty boy was caught
in the net of his own lies. 4. catch in a net:
to net a fish. net ted, net ting.
tion. They own a
grown, come, or mad
used; not worn or us
new cheese, new furnit
if new; fresh: to go
new potatoes
hat, āge, cãre, fär; let, bē, tėrm; it, īce; hot, ōpen, ôrder; oil, out; cup, pu̇t, rüle, ūse; takən

loneliness
(for octavio paz, li-young lee and chris tusa)

your hair is lost
in the forest
of ghosts

within this room
stars
raining down
a pink
mouth

birds drifting
in the flickering

loneliness

the shovel, leaning
leaning against the black air

the ground is cold
i can't recall our words

SOURCE TEXT
last dawn by octavio paz
eating alone by li-young lee
kindergarten portrait of my mother at mardi gras by chris tu

grown in my breast
(for william carlos williams, ezra pound, and james wright)

driven like hail
you are,
grown in my breast

on the long stair
of the seas
a pitiless light
has entered my hands

a snow that blinds us
has entered my hands

on the secret shores
the strange fowl provide for us
a home of songs

one suicide or another
their
branches grow out of me,
like arms

in my breast
the leaves flutter

half-stripped trees
struck by a wind together,
bending

outside my window just now
a small poem.

SOURCE TEXT
approach of winter by william carlos williams
a girl by ezra pound
a secret gratitude by james wright

phlox
476
pick
planation of the univer
guiding life. 4. calm
tude; accepting thi
are and making the b
phi los o phies.
phlox (floks), a comm
plant that has sh
clusters of various co
phoe be (fē/bi), a
can bird. See the pi
phone (fōn), teleph
phon ing.
pho net ic (fə net/ik
sounds made with
symbols are marks
ciation. We use TH
for the sound of th
or then.
pho no graph
(fō/nə graf), an
ment that records a
produces sounds.
phos pho rus
rəs), a chemical ele
that looks like yellow
Phosphorus burns
at ordinary temper
and shines in the
pho to (fō/tō),
graph. pho tos.
pho to graph
made wi
made
the
Phoebe (about 7 in. long)
Phonograph with one record playing and others in position to play in succession
education. 2. of matter; material: His
sical force was weak, but his mental and
al force was very great. The tide is a
sical force. 3. according to the laws of
ure: It is a physical impossibility for the
to rise in the west. 4. dealing with the
ral features of the earth. Physical
raphy teaches about the earth's for-
ion, climate, clouds, and tides.
i cal ly (fiz/ik li), in a physical
er; in physical respects; as regards
dy: After his vacation he was in fine
m both physically and mentally.
cian (fə zish/ən), doctor of med-
cist (fiz/ə sist), person who
much about physics.
ics (fiz/iks), the science that deals
matter and energy, and the action of
forms of energy. Physics studies
motion, heat, light, sound, and elec-
i ol o gy (fiz/i ol/ə ji), the science
with the normal working of living
or their organs: animal physiology,
physiology, vegetable physiology, the
ology of the blood.
sique (fə zēk/), body; bodily struc-
organization, or development: Samson
man of strong physique.
ist (pi an/ist or pē/ə nist), person
al instru-
wires.
hat
bird
square
or selec-
3. the best
of our
th the fingers;
flowers. 5. the
at one time. 6. a
oint for breaking
pickax. 7. a sharp-
phrased,
phys i cal
physical exer

i went into the neon fruit
(for allen ginsberg, charles bukowski, and emily dickinson)

the fish
they floated on the water,
too silver for dreaming

i stood watching the boat disappear
near the heavy drapes

i went into the neon fruit
supermarket

lights out in the
dreaming
blue automobiles

and stood watching the boat disappear

the picture window and
under the trees
a convenient grass

too silver for
dreaming
they floated on the water

they floated on the water,
their eyes still open,

was the saddest smile I ever saw

SOURCE TEXT
supermarket in california by allen ginsberg
a smile to remember by charles bukowski
a bird came down by emily dickinson

at five a.m. the tree has entered my hands
(for pablo neruda, ezra pound, and anne sexton)

your touch
the moonlight
has entered my hands

for the light and
we open the starry
branches grow out of me

in my inside out dream
you are, you are

life in the suburbs
leaves a little cathedral
for the light and the tree
has entered my hands,

and the tree
has entered my hands,
at five a.m.
at noon

praying to
my green ford
and the furniture and
the house
at five a.m.
at noon

i walk. i walk
as dark as the leathery eyes
i live in

SOURCE TEXT
a lemon by pablo naruda
a girl by ezra pound
45 mercy street by anne sexton

mallet 399 mangle
OOM
Man playing a mandolin

a window, into which everything
(for ee cummings, james wright, and hart crane)

be still.

do not dare breathe
the moon's
strange arranging and changing

shadow

its darkness
a window, into which
everything

without sound

the azure
a window, into which
everything

SOURCE TEXT
spring is like a perhaps hand by ee cummings
at melville's tomb by hart crane
beginning by james wright

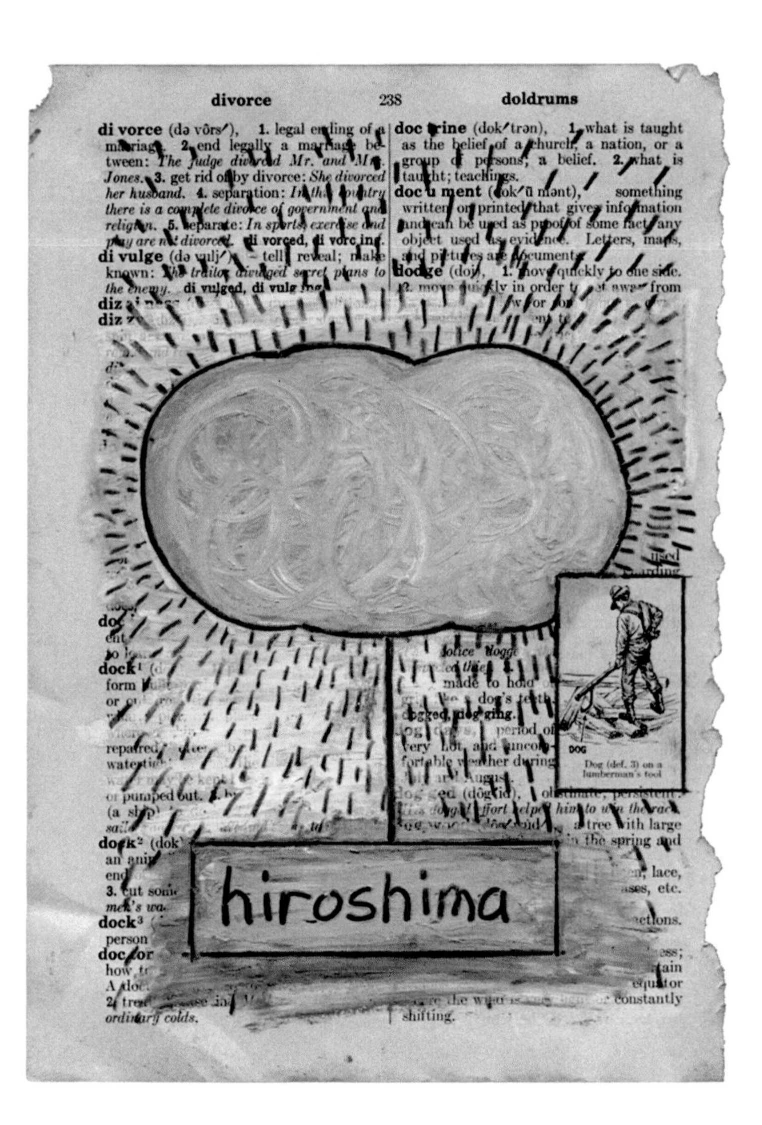
divorce 238 doldrums
hiroshima
DOG
Dog (def. 3) on a lumberman's tool

About the Author

George McKim was born in 1953 in Wilmington, North Carolina. He studied Fine Art Painting and received a BFA from Virginia Commonwealth University and an MFA from East Carolina University and attended Skowhegan School of Painting and Sculpture. His artwork has been exhibited in galleries and museums in the Southeast region in various group exhibitions. At the age of fifty-six, George began writing poetry. His poetry has been published or is forthcoming in *Diagram, The Found Poetry Review, Otoliths, Shampoo, elimae, GlitterMob, Dear Sir, Ditch, Cricket Online Review, Blaze Vox, Poets and Artists Magazine,* and other places.

Made in the USA
San Bernardino, CA
05 August 2015